FRUIT

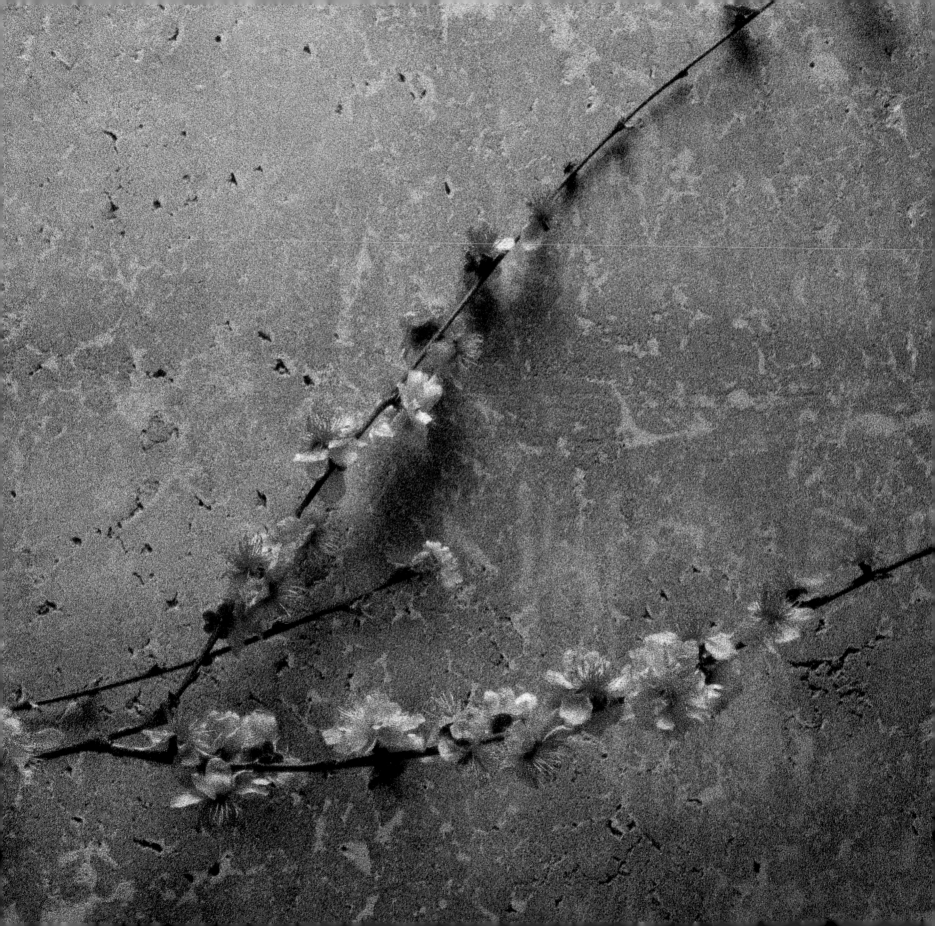

FRUIT

by Amy Nathan
Photographs by Kathryn Kleinman
Styling by Amy Nathan
Text by Jo Mancuso
Book design by Jacqueline Jones

Chronicle Books, San Francisco

Printed in Japan by Toppan Printing Co., Ltd.

Library of Congress Cataloging-in-Publication Data
Nathan, Amy.
    Fruit / Amy Nathan; photographs by Kathryn
    Kleinman.
        p.   cm.
    Bibliography: p.
    Includes index.
    ISBN 0-87701-556-2.
    ISBN 0-87701-444-2 (pbk.)
    1. Cookery (Fruit)   I. Kleinman, Kathryn.
    II. Title.
TX811.N37 1988
641.6'4—dc19   88-20230
                              CIP

Art direction: Amy Nathan and Kathryn Kleinman
Recipe and food assistance: Bob Lambert and
Stephanie Greenleigh
Photography assistance: Debra Casserly
Mechanical production: Suzanne Hidekawa, Terril
Neely, and Suzie Skugstad, Jacqueline Jones Design
Typography: Wilsted & Taylor

A portion of the poem "Lazy" by Lu Yu, which appeared
in One Hundred More Poems from the Chinese—
Love and the Turning Year by Kenneth Rexroth,
is reprinted here with permission from New Directions
Publishing Corporation, New York. © 1970 by
Kenneth Rexroth.
A quotation from Italian Food by Elizabeth David is
reprinted here with permission from Harper & Row,
Publishers, Inc., New York. © 1959, 1963, 1987 by
Elizabeth David.

Distributed in Canada by Raincoast Books
112 East Third Avenue, Vancouver, B.C. V5T 1C8
10 9 8 7 6 5 4 3 2 1

Chronicle Books
275 Fifth Street
San Francisco, California
94103

We wish to thank the following people for their efforts toward bringing this book to completion:

David Barich and Bill LeBlond for steering this book through the production channels at Chronicle Books.

Debra Casserly for her photographic assistance, organization, patience, and untiring work.

Susan DeVaty for her support, friendship, and willingness to be an extra pair of eyes.

Stephanie Greenleigh for her assistance, palate, dedication, and great energy.

Carolyn and Terry Harrison of Sonoma Antique Apple Nursery for their Pink Pearl and other special apples.

Michael Hodgson for his continued and generous support.

J. R. Brooks Co. for their help with exotic fruit.

Laura Jerrard for her assistance.

Iris Johnson for her grapevines, persimmons, and other flora from her garden.

Jacqueline Jones for her beautiful design of the book.

Bob Lambert for his help with recipe ideas, development, and testing.

Jo Mancuso for her writing and her research of fruit lore.

Lisa Osta for her photo assistance.

Nora Pate for her unusual cement bowls.

Tony Pisacane for his lemon branches.

Buddy Rhodes for his exquisite backgrounds.

Sharon Silva for her copyediting.

Suzie Skugstad and Suzanne Hidekawa for their design and production assistance.

Sara Slavin and Mark Steisel for their unending support.

Michaele Thunen for gathering the flowering fruit branches.

Peg Vasilak for her help with starfruit.

Warren Weber and Michael Schwab for their love and support.

Amy Nathan
Kathryn Kleinman

I've heard it said that it is in the vegetables that a chef expresses his or her personality. The same is true, I think, for fruit. ¶ In many ways, fruit is the most difficult subject I have approached. It seemed so perfect to me on its own. To enjoy it, so little needed to be done, yet it also afforded so many possibilities. I approached it with awe, reverence, humor, and experimentation. I learned that there is so much more to learn—particularly now when an interest in antique and heirloom varieties is growing, and when importers and domestic growers unveil more exotics each season. In many ways I had stepped into a new world. ¶ I have a vivid recollection of the enchantment I felt the first time I smelled a pineapple guava. I recall the awe that overtook me as I cut into my first pineapple quince. There was something about the simplicity and perfection of fruit that calmed me. Nature had really done it all. ¶ So, herewith an exploration into the various aspects of fruit: its beauty, simplicity, sensuality, variety, form, and flavors.

Amy Nathan

SAVORY BAKED APPLE WITH PORT WINE SAUCE

3 ounces shallots (about 4),
  coarsely chopped

1 tablespoon unsalted butter

1/2 pound ground pork

1/2 pound ground veal

1/4 cup brandy

1 teaspoon minced fresh thyme

Salt and freshly ground pepper
  to taste

4 large baking apples

4 whole spinach leaves

Port Wine Sauce (recipe follows)

□ In a skillet, sauté shallots in butter until translucent. Crumble pork and veal into skillet and sauté until browned. Drain off excess fat. Add brandy, thyme, salt, and pepper and cook until alcohol has evaporated.

□ Cut a 1-inch "cap" from the top of each apple; reserve caps. Using a melon baller, hollow out core and some of the flesh of the apples.

□ Fill each cavity with one-fourth of the meat mixture and top with a spinach leaf. Replace caps and arrange apples in a shallow baking pan.

□ Bake in a preheated 350 degree oven for 20 to 30 minutes, or until apples are tender yet firm enough to hold their shape. Spoon a pool of Port Wine Sauce onto individual serving plates. Top with apples and serve. Serves 4.

PORT WINE SAUCE

1 1/2 cups port wine

1 stick cinnamon

1 cup veal or beef brown stock

1 teaspoon cornstarch

1 teaspoon fresh lemon juice

1 teaspoon honey

□ Heat wine and cinnamon to boiling. Reduce heat and simmer for 5 minutes. Remove cinnamon. Add stock.

□ Dissolve cornstarch in lemon juice and stir into wine mixture. Bring to a boil, reduce heat, and simmer for 5 minutes. Stir in honey and serve. Makes 1 1/2 cups.

EASY UNBAKED APPLE TART

2 medium baking apples,
 peeled and cored
1/4 cup fresh lemon juice
3/4 cup ricotta cheese
3/4 cup cream cheese, softened
2 tablespoons honey
1 9-inch Whole-Wheat Pastry Crust,
 blind baked and cooled
 (recipe follows)
1/4 cup raisins
1 tablespoon unflavored gelatin
1/4 cup water
1 cup apple juice

□ Steam apples for 5 minutes. Cool slightly, slice thinly, and coat slices with lemon juice. Set aside.

□ With a wooden spoon, blend together ricotta, cream cheese, and honey until smooth. Spread cheese mixture in baked crust.

□ Drain apples and arrange slices, overlapping them, on top of the cheese mixture. Place raisins on apples in a pattern that pleases you.

□ Sprinkle gelatin over water. Let stand for 5 minutes to soften.

□ In a small saucepan, combine apple juice and gelatin mixture and heat slowly to boiling, stirring to dissolve gelatin. Remove from heat and cool until mixture just begins to thicken. Brush over fruit. Chill. Serves 6 to 8.

WHOLE-WHEAT PASTRY CRUST

1/4 pound (1 stick) unsalted butter,
 chilled
1 cup whole-wheat pastry flour
1/3 cup ground walnuts or almonds
1/4 cup apple juice, chilled

□ Cut butter into 8 equal pieces.

□ In a food processor fitted with a metal blade, combine flour, nuts, and butter. Process until mixture is the consistency of coarse meal.

□ Add apple juice in a steady stream and process until dough forms a ball (about 1 1/2 minutes).

□ Wrap in waxed paper and refrigerate for 30 minutes.

□ On a lightly floured board, roll dough into a 10-inch circle. Transfer to a 9-inch tart pan. Press dough firmly into pan. Prick base in several places with a fork. Wrap in waxed paper and freeze for 30 minutes.

□ Bake in a preheated 375 degree oven for approximately 15 minutes, or until lightly browned. Cool on a wire rack. Makes 1 9-inch pastry crust.

Pippin Apple

Bell Flower Apple

Crab Apple

Cox's Orange Pippin Apple

Red Rose Apple

Pink Pearl Apple

Winter Banana Apple

Red Delicious Apple

Red Rose Apple

Comfort me with apples,

for I am sick of love.

The Bible, Song of Solomon, c. 200

The apple is the fruit that stands for all fruits, the appellation given nearly every fruit in antiquity until it was granted a name of its own. According to Greek myth, an apple started the Trojan War, when Paris presented it to Aphrodite "the fairest," angering those slighted. ¶ The apple's seemingly unremarkable journey from tree to ground struck Isaac Newton with the notion of gravity. ¶ Horace advised eating only those apples picked by the light of the waning moon. ¶ The apple is responsible for some of our "homiest," most familiar foods, such as applesauce, apple cider, apple pie, crisp, tart, and cobbler. ¶ Pomologists say that if you shake the all-American McIntosh, the seeds may be heard to rattle. ¶ In the late nineteenth century, 320 apple varieties grew in North America; today perhaps a dozen are commonly sold at market. A renewed interest in "antique flavors" has inspired a resurgence of such varieties as the aromatic Cox's Orange Pippin; the orange-blushed Mutsu; the large, crunchy Winter Banana; and the tender, crisp Api, or Lady, a deep, glossy crimson on creamy yellow.

MIXED BERRIES WITH HYSSOP AND VANILLA CREAM

½ pint raspberries

½ pint blackberries

½ pint blueberries

½ pint olallie berries

1 ½ cups whipping cream

¼ cup honey

1 vanilla bean

20 fresh hyssop leaves

☐ Rinse berries and drain well. Toss together.

☐ Combine cream and honey.

☐ Soften vanilla bean in very hot water. Split and scrape out seeds into cream mixture. Stir to distribute evenly.

☐ Spoon a pool of cream onto individual serving plates. Top with berry mixture. Garnish with hyssop leaves. Serves 4.

TWO COLOR RASPBERRY BAVARIAN

1 tablespoon unflavored gelatin

1/4 cup water

1/3 cup honey

1 cup whipping cream

2 teaspoons framboise liqueur

3/4 cup plain yogurt

1 cup red raspberry purée

1/4 cup golden raspberry purée

Garnish:

Fresh mint leaves

Red and golden raspberries

□ Sprinkle gelatin over water. Let stand for 5 minutes to soften.

□ In a small saucepan, combine gelatin mixture with honey and heat to boiling, stirring to dissolve gelatin. Remove from heat, cool slightly, and whisk in cream.

□ In a bowl, whisk framboise into yogurt, then gradually beat in honey-cream mixture. Divide mixture in half.

□ Strain 3/4 cup of the red raspberry purée and set aside. Stir the remaining 1/4 cup red raspberry purée into one-half of the cream mixture. Stir golden raspberry purée into remaining cream mixture. Divide white purée evenly among 4 3/4-cup baba au rhum molds. Then divide pink purée evenly among the molds. Chill 4 hours.

□ Spoon a pool of the reserved raspberry purée onto individual serving plates. Dip each mold briefly in warm water and invert onto the raspberry purée. Garnish with mint leaves and raspberries. Serves 4.

Strawberry

On strawberries:
Doubtless God could have
made a better berry,
but doubtless God never did.
William Butler, 1600

According to Seneca Indian legend, strawberries grow beside the heavenly road. Mortals would not have had them if the sky woman, in falling through the hole in the celestial island, had not grasped at the edges and brought a vine down with her. ¶ Blackberries, dewberries, raspberries, loganberries, and strawberries wear their seeds on the outside, instead of burying them deep inside like most fruits. ¶ Tangling with thorny, arched canes, the picker of jet-beaded blackberries is often an on-the-spot consumer. The ripest sun-swollen berries, some as big as your thumb, are to lean and stretch for, at the top of the scratchy briars. The payoff is the delight of squashing the plump, inky-dark morsels against the roof of the mouth with the tongue.

CHOCOLATE SHORTCAKE WITH COCOA CREAM

Biscuits:

1 1/2 cups flour

1/2 cup unsweetened cocoa powder

1/3 cup granulated sugar

2 1/2 teaspoons baking powder

1/4 teaspoon salt

4 tablespoons unsalted butter, chilled

2/3 cup half and half

1 tablespoon sour cream

Filling:

1/4 cup superfine granulated sugar

1/4 cup unsweetened cocoa powder

1/2 teaspoon vanilla extract

2 cups whipping cream

1 pint strawberries, hulled and sliced

Garnish:

2 additional strawberries,
    halved lengthwise

Chocolate curls

□ Prepare biscuits: Sift together flour, cocoa, sugar, baking powder, and salt. Cut butter into small bits, then cut into dry ingredients with a pastry blender until mixture is the consistency of coarse meal. Combine half and half and sour cream and add to dough mixture. Mix well.

□ Knead dough gently on a lightly floured board until smooth. Shape the dough into a cylinder about 3 inches long and 3 inches in diameter. Slice cylinder into 4 equal discs.

□ Lay discs on a greased baking sheet and bake in a preheated 400 degree oven for 10 to 12 minutes. Cool on a wire rack.

□ Prepare filling: Whisk together sugar and cocoa. Combine cocoa mixture with vanilla and whipping cream and beat until stiff peaks form.

□ To assemble: Split each biscuit into 2 equal layers and set top layer aside. Arrange strawberry slices over biscuit base. Pipe whipped cream over sliced berries. Top with another layer of sliced berries and then with the top biscuit layer. Pipe a rosette of whipped cream on top. Garnish with a strawberry half and chocolate curls. Serve immediately. Serves 4.

STRAWBERRY-RHUBARB COMPOTE

1 pound rhubarb, trimmed and sliced
into 1-inch lengths

½ cup strawberry juice

⅓ cup honey

1½ cups whipping cream

1 tablespoon confectioners' sugar

½ cup cassis liqueur

2 strawberries, halved lengthwise

□ Place the rhubarb in a single layer in a nonreactive sauté pan.

□ Pour in strawberry juice, bring to a boil, and simmer 3 to 6 minutes, until pieces have softened but not lost their shape. Length of cooking time is dependent on maturity of fruit.

□ Remove from heat and stir in honey. Chill.

□ Whip cream with confectioners' sugar until soft peaks form.

□ Place a "pillow" of whipped cream in the center of individual serving plates. Top with compote. Drizzle 2 tablespoons cassis around perimeter of cream. Garnish with strawberry half. Serve immediately. Serves 4.

B ERRY-
FLAVORED VODKAS

¹/₂ cup blueberries

¹/₂ cup raspberries

³/₄ cup strawberries,

. hulled and quartered

6 cups vodka

□ In 3 separate containers, combine
each fruit with 2 cups vodka.
Cover and let stand at room
temperature for at least 2 days.
Remove fruit. Serve vodka
well chilled. Makes 6 cups.

CHERRY

CHERRY PECAN CAKE

2 eggs, well beaten

1 cup granulated sugar

1 teaspoon vanilla extract

1 cup flour, sifted

1 teaspoon baking powder

½ teaspoon salt

¾ cup chopped pecans

2 cups pitted
　　sweet or sweet/sour cherries

1 cup sweetened whipped cream

Cherry Sauce:

1 tablespoon unsalted butter

2 cups cherry juice

1 tablespoon granulated sugar

2 tablespoons cornstarch,
　　blended with 2 tablespoons water

1 tablespoon fresh lemon juice

Garnish:

A few additional pitted cherries

2 tablespoons chopped pecans

□ Beat together eggs, sugar, and vanilla.

□ Combine flour, baking powder, salt, and pecans. Fold into egg mixture.

□ Pour one-third of the batter into a greased 9-inch cake pan.

□ Mix two-thirds of the cherries into the remaining batter. Pour it evenly over the bottom layer of batter. Top with the remaining cherries.

□ Bake in a preheated 350 degree oven for 45 minutes.

□ Prepare sauce: Melt butter in a small saucepan. Add cherry juice, sugar, and cornstarch mixture and stir over medium heat until sauce begins to thicken. Do not boil. Add lemon juice and stir a few minutes.

□ Remove cake to wire rack to cool. Slice into wedges and serve with warm sauce and whipped cream. Garnish with additional cherry halves and chopped pecans, if desired. Serves 6.

Bing Cherry

Only the incautious buy cherries before nibbling. Sweet varieties are interchangeable in recipes, but sour Montmorencies and Morellos—rather tart to enjoy fresh—are prized for pies, preserves, and savory sauces. Relish the best melding of sweet and sour in Duke cherries. ¶ The sweet cherry is known as *Prunus avium*, "bird's plum," for blackbirds or robins are wont to harvest the just-ripening crop on the wing, before land-based pickers can pluck the splendid, glossy "hearts" and savor their dense flesh. ¶ "Life is just a bowl of cherries" suggests bright, tender morsels heaped elegantly for the taking. ¶ Thirty-five hundred cherry trees grace Washington, D.C., a 1912 gift from the people of Tokyo to the people of the United States. Japan's Cherry Blossom Festival dates back to A.D. 812, when the upper classes of Kyoto gathered for "blossom viewing" parties at the imperial court of Emperor Saga. An important symbol to the Japanese people, the cherry blossom's appearance marks the onset of the ancient rite of spring; to samurai, it represented the ephemeral glory of the spirit.

CITRUS SALAD WITH AVOCADO CREAM AND BLEU CHEESE WAFERS

2 oranges

1 white grapefruit

1 pink or red grapefruit

A few pomegranate seeds for garnish

Bleu Cheese Wafers (recipe follows)

Avocado Cream:

1 ripe avocado

1 tablespoon fresh lime juice

1/2 cup crème fraîche

1 1/2 cups milk

□ Peel and segment oranges and grapefruits. Place segments on paper toweling to drain.

□ Prepare cream: Peel and pit avocado. In a blender or food processor, combine avocado and lime juice. Add crème fraîche and milk and blend until smooth.

□ Spoon a pool of cream onto individual serving plates. Arrange a circle of citrus segments over cream, alternating colors. Sprinkle with pomegranate seeds. Serve with Bleu Cheese Wafers.

Serves 4.

BLEU CHEESE WAFERS

1/4 pound (1 stick) unsalted butter, softened

1/2 pound bleu cheese, crumbled

1 cup flour

1/4 teaspoon baking powder

Dash salt

□ With a spatula or wooden spoon, blend together butter and bleu cheese.

□ Combine flour, baking powder, and salt. With a pastry blender, cut in butter mixture to form a dough.

□ Divide dough into 4 equal parts. Roll each part into a cylinder 4 inches long and 1 1/2 inches in diameter. Cover with waxed paper and chill until firm.

□ Cut cylinders into 1/3-inch-thick slices and arrange on a parchment-lined baking sheet. Bake in a preheated 375 degree oven for 15 to 18 minutes, or until golden. Cool on baking sheet for 10 minutes, then transfer to wire rack to cool completely. Makes 4 dozen.

COLD TANGERINE SOUFFLÉ

3 tablespoons unflavored gelatin

½ cup water

5 eggs, separated

⅔ cup granulated sugar

Grated zest of 2 organic tangerines

⅔ cup frozen tangerine juice
    concentrate, thawed

2 cups whipping cream

Garnish:

White chocolate curls

Tangerine zest curls

□ Sprinkle gelatin over water. Let stand for 5 minutes to soften.

□ In a small saucepan, slowly heat gelatin mixture to boiling, stirring to dissolve gelatin. Remove from heat and cool slightly.

□ Beat together the egg yolks and sugar. Stir in zest and juice concentrate.

□ Whip cream until soft peaks form. Fold into tangerine mixture. Stir in gelatin and continue stirring until mixture begins to thicken.

□ Beat egg whites until stiff. Gently fold into tangerine mixture.

□ Collar a 1½-quart soufflé dish with greased waxed paper.

□ Spoon mixture into soufflé dish. Chill 4 hours.

□ Remove collar and garnish with white chocolate curls and tangerine zest. Serves 6.

LEMON
POUSSIN WITH SAVORY LEMON MOUSSE

3 organic lemons

2 fresh poussins

4 to 6 garlic cloves

6 stale bread cubes

4 tablespoons unsalted butter

Savory Lemon Mousse
 (recipe follows)

Garnish:

A few sprigs of thyme and savory

Pineapple sage blossoms

Society chive blossoms

□ Cut 1 lemon into ½-inch-thick half rounds. Save ends. Cut remaining 2 lemons in half to squeeze for juice.

□ Rub outside of poussins with the lemon "ends" and then with a clove of garlic. Squeeze juice from ½ lemon into cavity of each poussin. Fill each cavity with half of the lemon slices, garlic cloves, and bread cubes and 1 tablespoon of the butter. Secure cavity opening closed with a toothpick or skewer.

□ Place poussins in a shallow baking pan. Squeeze juice from ½ lemon over all. Dot with remaining 2 tablespoons of butter. Bake in a preheated 375 degree oven for 50 minutes, squeezing juice of remaining lemon half over poussins 3 times during baking.

□ Split poussins in half and serve each half with some of the "stuffing" and Savory Lemon Mousse. Garnish with herb sprigs and blossoms. Serves 4.

SAVORY LEMON MOUSSE

1 teaspoon unflavored gelatin

⅓ cup fresh lemon juice

Zest of 1 organic lemon, minced

3 tablespoons granulated sugar

1 teaspoon minced fresh savory

2 teaspoons minced fresh thyme

1 cup whipping cream

□ Sprinkle gelatin over 1 tablespoon of the lemon juice. Let stand for 5 minutes to soften.

□ In a small saucepan, combine the gelatin mixture and the remaining lemon juice and heat slowly to boiling, stirring to dissolve gelatin.

□ Add zest, sugar, savory, and thyme and stir to dissolve sugar. Remove from heat and refrigerate while whipping cream.

□ Whip cream until soft peaks form. Gently fold in lemon-gelatin mixture. Chill. Makes 2 cups.

LIME SOUP

4 cups chicken broth

2 chicken breast halves,
*   skin removed*

1/3 cup alphabet pasta .

1/3 cup chopped red onion

1/4 cup fresh lime juice
*   (1 to 2 limes)*

1/3 cup chopped fresh Italian parsley

1 small ripe avocado, peeled, pitted,
*   and sliced*

□ In a saucepan, bring broth to a boil. Add chicken, reduce to simmer, cover, and cook 20 minutes. Remove chicken from broth. Cool slightly, then pull meat off the bones and shred. Set aside.

□ Reheat broth to boiling. Add pasta, reduce heat to a low boil, cover, and cook for 10 minutes.

□ Add onion, lime juice, chicken, parsley, and avocado. Cover and simmer for 5 minutes.

Serves 4.

Lime

Yellow Grapefruit

Lemon

Meyer Lemon

Kumquat

Pink Grapefruit

Tangerine

Tangelo

Navel Orange

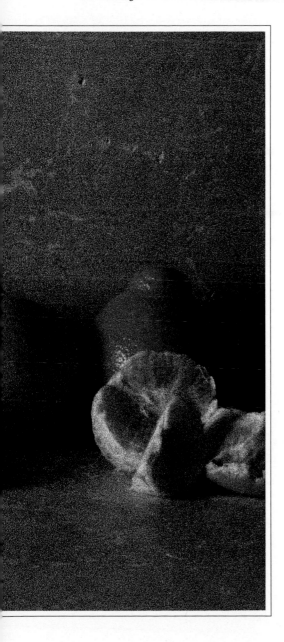

*A grapefruit
is a lemon that had a chance
and took advantage of it.*

Anonymous

Mandarin Orange

The citrus is neat and thoughtful, the only fruit that arranges itself in edible segments. Juicy pulp is packaged in delicate partitioning membrane, the plump crescents offering only a gentle, clinging resistance when pried carefully apart. Beneath smooth or pebbly skin, plush strings and a web of "rag" wrap protectively around the tight cluster. ¶ "Loose-skinned oranges" are forever causing confusion: the complexly perfumed mandarin and its hybrids, including the tangerine; the tangelo, born of mandarin and grapefruit; the rumpled-skinned ugli; and the new lavender gem, luscious cross between grapefruit and tangerine. ¶ Other branches of the citrus family tree hang heavy with the piercing lime; the puckery lemon; the great globe grapefruit; the tart-sweet pomelo, dryish—almost squeaky—inside; and the tiny kumquat, edible in its entirety, with sweet, spongy rind and sharp-flavored pulp. ¶ In her story "Borderland," M. F. K. Fisher pondered secret eating pleasures as she wrote of tangerines: the delicate sections first heated on the radiator, then chilled on the snow-packed sill outside her Strasbourg window.

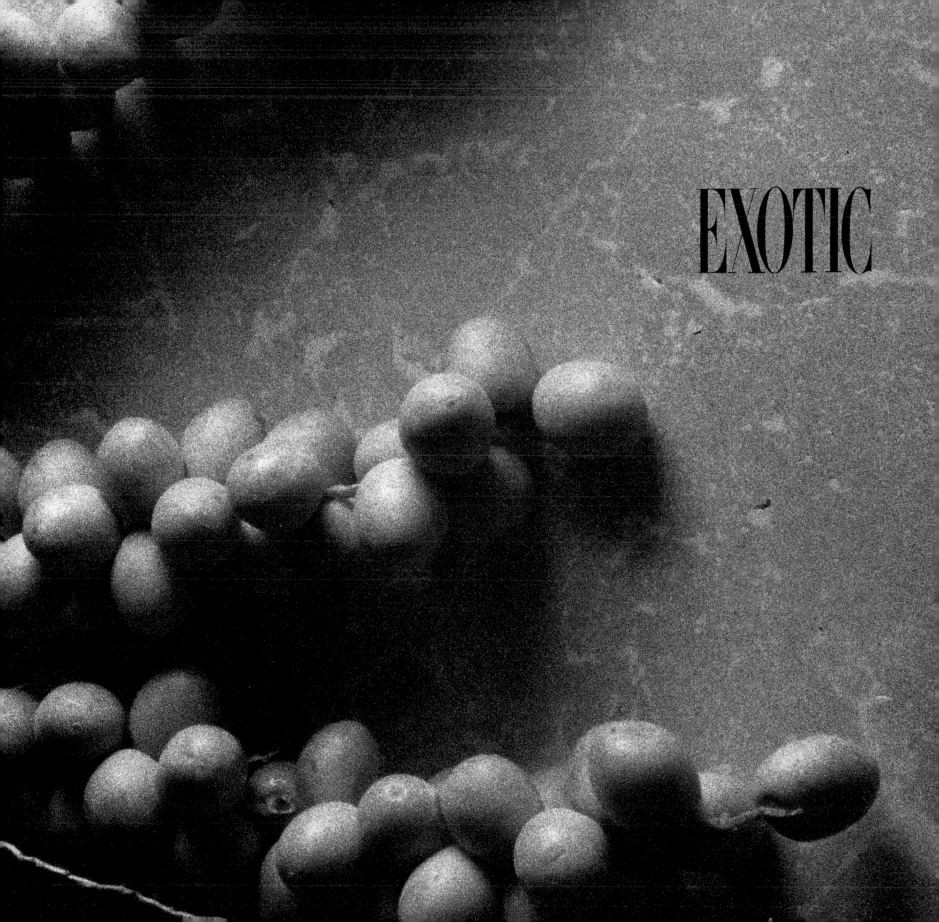

PEAR APPLE WITH PÂTÉ AND RED CURRANTS

To compose a simple appetizer plate, accompany a slice of duck or chicken liver pâté with a few slices of chilled pear apple and a sprig or two of red currants. The crunch and sweetness of the pear apple provide a crisp base for the pâté; the tartness of the currants contrasts with the richness of the other flavors.

Tamarillo   *Golden Tamarillo*

Fruit, as it was our primitive,

and most excellent as well as

most innocent food,

whilst it grew in Paradise;

a climate so benign,

and a soil so richly impregnated

with all that the influence of Heaven

could communicate to it;

so it has still preserved,

and retained no small tincture

of its original and celestial virtue.

John Evelyn
Compleat Gard'ner, 1693

Coconut Spoonbread with Exotic Fruits

Spoonbread:

½ cup whipping cream

1⅔ cups coconut milk

¼ cup granulated sugar

¼ teaspoon salt

¾ cup white cornmeal

1 cup sweetened shredded coconut

4 eggs, separated

1 teaspoon baking powder

Fruit:

1 large very ripe cherimoya,
   puréed until smooth

1 kiwi, peeled and
   sliced into half rounds

1 pepino, peeled, seeded,
   and sliced

1 pineapple guava,
   peeled and sliced into julienne strips

Garnish:

Toasted coarsely shredded coconut

□ Prepare spoonbread: In a medium saucepan, bring the cream, coconut milk, sugar, and salt to a boil, stirring to dissolve sugar.

□ Remove from the heat. Stir in the cornmeal and shredded coconut.

□ Stir a little of the cornmeal mixture into the egg yolks. Beat in the baking powder. Return to the main mixture.

□ Beat egg whites to the soft peak stage, then gently fold into the cornmeal mixture.

□ Turn into a buttered 2-quart soufflé dish. Bake in a preheated 350 degree oven for 25 minutes.

□ Serve warm or cool. Using a large spoon, scoop some of the spoonbread onto individual serving plates. Spoon a pool of cherimoya purée next to the spoonbread. Surround with suggested exotic fruits or others, as desired. Sprinkle with toasted coconut. Serves 4.

Pineapple Guava

Fruits of intrigue,

these exotics:

Mysterious shapes,

Scents so sweet

that I must inhale

again and again;

I close my eyes

and am transported.

Curiosity overcomes me;

I cut one open to reveal

the wonder of Nature.

A.N.

STARFRUIT SAMPLER

1 pint strawberries, hulled

2 tablespoons granulated sugar

2 starfruits, sliced crosswise

2 slices crystalized ginger,
    finely chopped

1/4 cup macadamia nuts,
    chopped and toasted

1/4 cup rose petals, cut into strips

□ Rinse the strawberries and drain
well. Toss with the sugar. Let stand
for 30 minutes. Purée and strain.

□ Spoon a pool of berry purée onto
individual serving plates. Set
starfruit slices over purée. Place
some of the ginger, macadamia
nuts, and rose petals around purée.
Serve immediately. Serves 4.

Pepino

Cape Gooseberry

Kiwi Fruit

Passion Fruit

Pear Apple

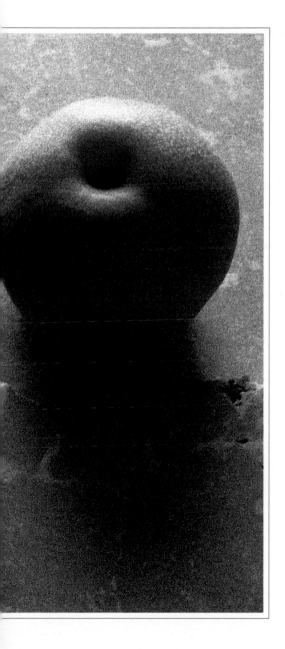

Here the currants red and white
In yon green bush at her sight
Peep through their
shady leaves, and cry
Come eat me, as she passes by.

Robert Heath
Clarastella, 1650

The global produce crate brims with all manner of "new" fruits both exquisite and intriguing, many making the journey from New Zealand. Their appearance may amuse and perplex: The cherimoya resembles a green grenade. The perfumed passion fruit looks like a dried-up dark-purple golf ball. ¶ Nomenclature and family ties veil their natures further, drawing us into a delicious detective game. The Chinese gooseberry is no relation to the gooseberry; New Zealand exporters renamed it the kiwi. The Cape gooseberry, with a parchment wrapper that may be pulled back and twisted into a holder, is not a gooseberry at all, but a ground cherry. Nor is the tutti-frutti–flavored pineapple guava a true guava; in fact, the guava itself is a berry. Also a berry, but with only a single seed, is the date. ¶ It is in aroma and flavor that the mystery of exotic fruits deepens and beckons irresistibly. The creamy cherimoya evokes banana and pineapple, mango and papaya. The passion fruit's heady fragrance combines lemon, jasmine, and honey. And star-shaped slices of the waxy-skinned carambola (starfruit) suggest grape, apple, and plum.

FIG

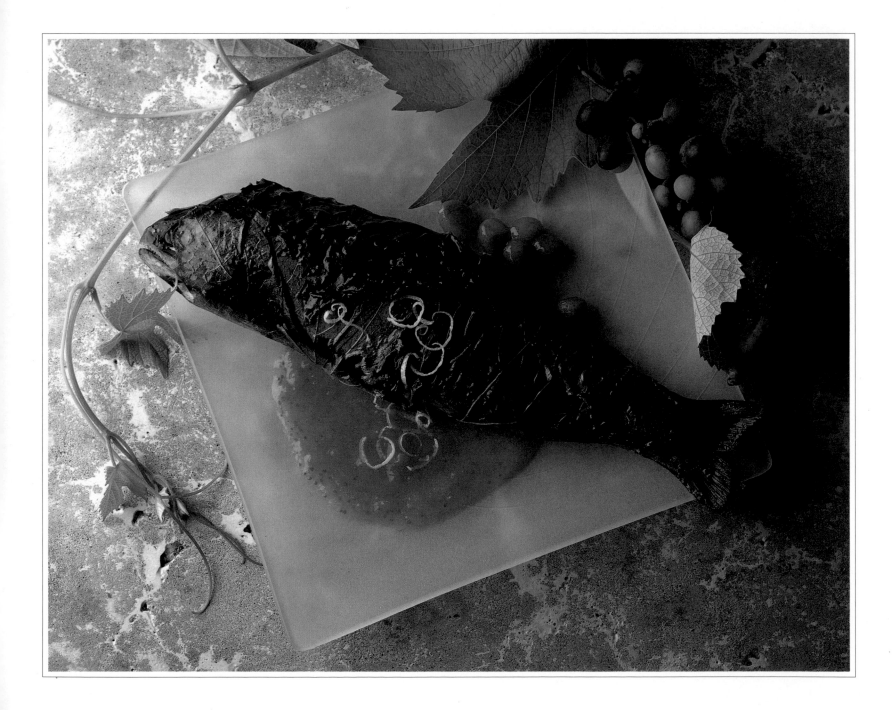

**L**EMON
FIG SAUCE

2 tablespoons unsalted butter

Generous ½ cup chopped figs

   (approximately 6 large or 8 small)

½ cup sake

3 tablespoons fresh lemon juice

Grated zest of organic lemon to taste

□ Melt butter in a medium skillet.
Sauté figs for 2 minutes. Add sake.

□ Cook over medium heat until
mixture thickens to the consistency
to coat a spoon (approximately
3 minutes).

□ Stir in lemon juice. Sprinkle sauce
with lemon zest when serving. A
nice complement to grilled fish
or roast pork. Serves 2.

FIG GRATIN

6 to 8 figs, cut into

⅜-inch-thick slices

½ cup whipping cream

1 egg yolk

1½ tablespoons honey

1 tablespoon bourbon

½ teaspoon freshly grated nutmeg

□ Arrange sliced figs in a single layer in 1 large or 4 small individual au gratin dishes.

□ Whisk together cream, egg yolk, honey, bourbon, and nutmeg. Pour over sliced figs.

□ Broil 1 inch from flame for 4 to 5 minutes until browned and bubbly. Serve immediately. Serves 4.

Black Mission Fig

Until modern times, the fig, the grapevine, the olive tree, and the wheat stalk supplied Mediterranean cultures with most of their food. Ancient Greeks thought figs so healthful that they were part of the athletes' diet for the original Olympic Games. ¶ Figs cloak themselves in many hues. The Mission is purple-black; the small Kadota is a translucent green or yellow; the Adriatic has light green skin and dark pink flesh; the large, squat Calimyrna—the Turkish Smyrna transplanted to California—has a smooth, thick skin, yellowish green, sometimes ambered. ¶ Although it resembles a faintly leathery pouch, the thin-skinned fig is highly perishable, so drying is common. Figs grown in the hanging gardens of Babylon were preserved by burying them in hot desert sands. ¶ The fig is the most sensual and secretive of fruits. The poet André Gide wrote of the fig's hidden loves, its flowering folded away. The tree bears no external blossoms; the flower grows inside the fruit. What is eaten is the fleshy receptacle and the pulpy mass that develops around the "preserved" bloom within.

FIGS WITH ICE CREAM AND SARSAPARILLA SAUCE

2 cups vanilla ice cream,
    softened for scooping
4 white figs
8 black figs
Sarsaparilla Sauce (recipe follows)
4 pecan halves
Praline Stars for garnish,
    optional (recipe follows)

□ In advance, scoop ice cream into
4 ½-cup molds. Freeze until very
firm, usually 4 hours. Unmold
by briefly dipping mold into warm
water and then inverting onto
waxed paper. Return ice cream
to freezer.

□ Trim stems from figs and cut a
deep X into each fig from the top.
Push up slightly from bases to
expose flesh.

□ Spoon a pool of Sarsaparilla
Sauce onto individual serving plates.
Arrange 2 black figs and 1 white fig
atop sauce on each plate and set ice
cream mold alongside. Dip a
pecan half in remaining sauce and
set atop ice cream. Garnish with
Praline Stars, if desired. Serves 4.

SARSAPARILLA SAUCE

2 tablespoons water
1 cup granulated sugar
½ cup apple juice
½ teaspoon root beer flavoring

□ Put water in a saucepan and
sprinkle sugar over it. Cook over
high heat without stirring until
water has evaporated and sugar
turns golden brown. Be extremely
careful when caramelizing the
sugar, as it reaches far higher
temperatures than boiling water
and can cause severe burns.

□ Remove from heat and stir to
dissolve any remaining sugar
crystals. Allow to cool for
5 minutes.

□ Slowly pour apple juice into sugar
and then stir in root beer flavoring.
Return to heat and stir constantly
to dissolve sugar in juice. Cool.
Makes ¾ cup.

PRALINE STARS

2 tablespoons water
1 cup granulated sugar

□ Put water in a saucepan and
sprinkle sugar over it. Cook over
high heat without stirring until
water has evaporated and sugar
turns golden brown.

□ Meanwhile, select cookie
cutters in the shape of small stars.
Lightly oil the cutters and arrange
them on a baking sheet lined with
waxed paper.

□ Pour hot caramelized sugar into
the cookie cutters. Cool completely
to set pralines. Unmold carefully.
Makes 4.

GRAPE

GRAPES
IN WINE ASPIC

8 tablespoons unflavored gelatin

2 cups water

4 cups white wine grape juice
(such as Riesling or Gewürtztraminer)

1½ cups grapes of assorted varieties

□ Sprinkle gelatin over water. Let stand for 5 minutes to soften.

□ In a medium saucepan, combine gelatin mixture and grape juice and heat slowly to boiling, stirring to dissolve gelatin.

□ Remove from heat and pour half of the mixture into a 9-by-13-inch pan. Chill until set (approximately 1 hour). Reserve remainder of mixture in a warm spot.

□ If grapes are large, cut in half lengthwise. Arrange grapes over chilled gelatin in a pattern that pleases you.

□ Pour reserved gelatin mixture carefully over grape pattern. (If mixture has set, warm slightly by setting pan in a bowl of hot water until mixture resumes liquid state.) Chill until firm (approximately 3 hours).

□ To serve, slice into rectangles and remove from pan with a thin flat spatula. Serves 4.

ARCHITECTURAL SALAD WITH APRICOT RIESLING SAUCE

8 tablespoons unflavored gelatin

2 cups water

2 cups white grape juice

2 cups red grape juice

1 ripe persimmon

Apricot Riesling Sauce
(recipe follows)

A few fresh hyssop leaves

□ Sprinkle gelatin over water. Let stand for 5 minutes to soften, then divide mixture in half.

□ Place the white grape juice in a small saucepan and the red grape juice in another. Add half of the gelatin mixture to each pan and heat slowly to boiling, stirring to dissolve gelatin.

□ Pour each juice mixture into a shallow 8-inch-square pan. Chill until set (approximately 1 hour).

□ Slice set gelatin layers into 1½-inch cubes. Arrange cubes in architectural "towers" on individual serving plates.

□ Peel persimmon and cut into ¼-inch-thick half rounds. Cut 4 of the half rounds in half to form triangular "pediments." Set persimmons atop gelatin "columns" as shown in photograph.

□ Spoon a pool of the Apricot Riesling Sauce at the base of each "column." Scatter a few small hyssop leaves around the plate. Serves 4.

APRICOT RIESLING SAUCE

2 cups apricot nectar

¼ cup grey Riesling wine

Squeeze of fresh lime juice

□ In a large, flat, heavy pan placed over high heat, reduce the apricot nectar to ¾ cup, whisking occasionally to prevent burning. Chill, then stir in the wine and lime juice. Makes 1 cup.

Thompson Seedless Grape

Champagne Grape

Red Flame Grape

Ribier Grape

Grapes are ancient. They are depicted on Egyptian tombs, Roman murals, and Greek friezes. A jar labeled "unfermented grape juice" was discovered in the tomb of Tutankhamen. Most of the grapes we eat today are Old World varieties developed from a single species, *Vitis vinifera.* ¶ Everything on the grapevine is edible: the fruits themselves, seeds, leaves, young shoots, tendrils—even the sap tapped from the vine. We know that American Indians chewed on the branchlets and leaves to savor their pleasant taste. ¶ "Slip-skin" table grapes, so named because the pulp separates easily from the skin as you eat them, include the blackish-purple Concord with a silvery bloom or powder; the big purply-red Catawba; and the Delaware, small and pink. Wild grapes have been fitted with such names as canyon, chicken, downey, mustang, pinewood, rock, sand, scuppernong, silverleaf, sweet scented, and turkey. Wine grapes, like claret, Pinot white and black, gamay, and muscat, seldom translate well to the table. ¶ "Peel me a grape" and you will find white pulp. Black, red, or white, the skin gives the grape its color.

A drinker at table
was offered grapes for dessert.
"Much obliged," said he,
pushing the plate aside.
"I am not accustomed to taking
my wine in pills."
Jean Anthelme Brillat-Savarin

MANGO &
PAPAYA

MANGO WITH GINGER AND LIME

2 mangoes, peeled and cut
  into ½-inch cubes
1-inch piece ginger root, peeled and
  cut into very fine julienne strips
¼ cup tiny fresh mint leaves
Juice of 2 limes
Honeysuckle blossoms for garnish

□ Combine mangoes, ginger, and mint leaves. Add lime juice and toss well. Let stand for at least 30 minutes.

□ Serve at room temperature, garnished with a few honeysuckle blossoms. (Although honeysuckle blossoms are nontoxic, you may wish only to sip the nectar from the bases.) Serves 4.

Mango

Hindus revere the mango, and imbue it with mythical importance. Legend has it that the daughter of the sun fled from a wicked sorceress, later to emerge from the center of a mango. ¶ The mango has the coloration of an exotic tropical bird, with its skin of orange and red and a golden-yellow flesh. A relative of the cashew, poison ivy, and pepper tree, it has a taste that conjures memories of peach and pine, pear and apricot, melon and pineapple. ¶ In its native India, people eat a mango from the inside out. They knead the fruit ever so gently until the pulp is nearly liquified, remove the stem, and suck the juice out through the hole while squeezing carefully to avoid splitting the skin. ¶ Christopher Columbus observed in his journal that the natives of the West Indies were "very strong and live largely on a tree melon called the fruit of the angels." We know this as the papaya, of green, yellow, or orange skin, pink to orange flesh, a cavity massed with small, black edible seeds, and a sweet, mild, sometimes musky flavor.

PAPAYA-MINT SAMPLER

Mint Tea Sorbet (recipe follows)

1 papaya, peeled, seeded, and sliced

Mint Crêpes (recipe follows),

    rolled and cut into ³⁄₈-inch lengths

A few fresh mint leaves

□ To assemble each serving, place 1 scoop of sorbet in the center of each plate. Surround with papaya slices, crêpe spirals, and mint leaves. Serves 4.

MINT TEA SORBET

2 cups mellow mint tea

3 tablespoons honey

¼ cup fresh mint leaves,

    cut into julienne strips

1 egg white, beaten until foamy

□ Combine tea, honey, and mint leaves.

□ Stir in egg white.

□ Freeze in ice cream maker according to manufacturer's directions until set to scooping consistency. Scoop and serve immediately, or hold scoops in freezer until serving time. Makes 2 cups.

MINT CRÊPES

1 cup flour

3 eggs

1 tablespoon granulated sugar

1½ cups milk

¼ cup fresh mint leaves,

    cut into julienne strips

2 tablespoons unsalted butter

□ In a blender or food processor, combine flour, eggs, and sugar. With machine running, add milk in a slow, steady stream. Allow batter to rest in the refrigerator for 1 hour.

□ Remove batter from refrigerator and stir in mint.

□ Heat a 6-inch crêpe pan over medium heat. When hot, wipe the surface with a little of the butter. Wait for the butter to sizzle, then ladle in about 2 tablespoons batter. Immediately tilt the pan from side to side to spread the batter evenly and thinly over the bottom. Cook over medium heat until golden on the first side. Flip the crêpe and cook about 1 minute on the second side. Repeat with remaining batter, adding more butter to the pan as needed and stacking crêpes as they are cooked. Crêpes not needed for the sampler may be well wrapped and refrigerated or frozen for future use. Makes about 20.

HONEYED CHARENTAIS MELON

Select 1 small Charentais melon per person. Slice off top portion of melon to form a "cap." Remove and discard seeds. Fill each melon with ¼ cup Couchen (honey liqueur). Replace cap. Serve within 1 hour. If you cannot find a honey-flavored liqueur, Pineau de Charentes is a nice alternative.

SMOKED CHICKEN WITH HONEYDEW

2 whole smoked chicken breasts,
   boned and skin removed
½ honeydew melon
4 small fresh mozzarella cheese balls

□ Shred smoked chicken into
thin strips.

□ Peel and seed melon and cut into
¼-inch-thick slices. Cut one of
the slices into julienne strips.

□ On individual serving plates
mound one-fourth of the smoked
chicken. Top with some of the
julienned honeydew. Fan honeydew
slices next to chicken. Place
mozzarella alongside and serve.
Serves 4.

M
ELON
SORBETS WITH
TOMATO PURÉE

½ cantaloupe

½ honeydew

Lime-flavored carbonated water

Tomato Purée (recipe follows)

Savory sprigs and borage blossoms
   for garnish

□ Peel and seed melons. In a blender or food processor, purée cantaloupe. Add carbonated water to make 2 cups liquid and blend briefly. Freeze in ice cream maker according to manufacturer's directions until set to scooping consistency. Scoop and hold in freezer until ready to serve. Repeat procedure with honeydew.
□ Spoon a pool of Tomato Purée onto individual serving plates. Place 1 scoop of each flavor sorbet on the purée. Garnish with savory sprigs and borage blossoms. Serve immediately. Serves 4.

TOMATO PURÉE

12 Roma tomatoes, peeled
   and seeded

1 tablespoon Pernod liqueur

¼ teaspoon ground white pepper

□ In a blender or food processor combine all ingredients and purée until smooth. Makes 2 cups.

Cantaloupe

Casaba Melon

Persian Melon

Honeydew Melon

Crenshaw Melon

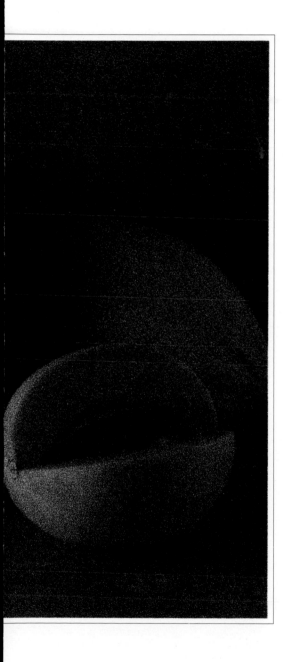

When one has tasted watermelons,
one knows what angels eat.
It was not a Southern watermelon
that Eve took;
we know it because she repented.
Mark Twain

Pink Honeydew Melon

All melons belong to the *Cucurbitaceae* family, which includes cucumbers, gourds, pumpkins, and squashes. ¶ An anonymous Arab saying assures that "He who fills his stomach with melons is like him who fills it with light—there is a blessing in it." ¶ Most melons are so obliging as to detach themselves from their stems when ripe. ¶ In the mid-1800s, Dr. David Livingston discovered watermelons growing wild in the remote interior of Africa. On long hunting treks through arid regions, tribesmen carried them like canteens, with their water-heavy pulp. ¶ Slices of watermelon are commonly sold from pushcarts on the sidewalks of Naples, where they are considered the only way to "eat, drink and wash your face at the same time." ¶ Melons are interchangeable in most recipes: cantaloupe, wrapped in a rough, cream-colored raised network; the "green whale of summer" watermelon, sometimes yellow-fleshed; mild and sweet Persians; round, green-streaked Charentais with fragrant orange flesh; Christmas melons like striped zeppelins; and winter melons such as the furrowed golden casaba and the hefty, sweet honeydew.

PEACH &
NECTARINE

SIMPLE
FRUIT CANAPÉS

Spread Kracklebread or other puffed crispbread cracker with cultured cream cheese or crème fraîche. Top with sliced peaches, nectarines, and plums. Serve immediately.

NECTARINES SUPREME

2 nectarines

½ cup ricotta cheese

2 tablespoons honey

Garnish:

Coarsely chopped hazelnuts

Black peppermint sprigs

□ Cut nectarines in half. Remove pits. Cut a small portion from the base of each nectarine half so that the fruit will sit flat; reserve small pieces.

□ Blend ricotta and honey with a spatula or wooden spoon.

□ Fill each nectarine half with 2 tablespoons of the ricotta mixture. Sprinkle with hazelnuts. Garnish with reserved nectarine pieces and peppermint sprigs. Serves 4.

Babcock Peach

Rightly thought of there is

poetry in peaches,

even when they are canned.

Harley Granville Barker
The Madras House, 1911

A member of the rose family, the juicy-fleshed peach has a downy skin like short-napped velvet, colored golden yellow with a rosy crimson blush. ¶ Auguste Renoir advised young artists to "first paint apples and peaches in a fruit bowl" before attempting the golden pink tones of the female breast. ¶ The peach has long been regarded by its original cultivators, the Chinese, as an emblem of immortality and symbol of friendship. Legend tells us of the Banto, which takes three thousand years to ripen and assures health, virility, and unending life to anyone fortunate enough to eat it. ¶ "Training is everything," wrote Mark Twain. "The peach was once a bitter almond. . . ." ¶ The highly colored nectarine is not a fuzzless cross between peach and plum, but a member of the peach clan. Apparently confused about its exact place on the family tree, it may be found growing on the same tree—though on different branches—within arm's reach of its downier relations. And if you plant its pits, you may or may not get nectarines.

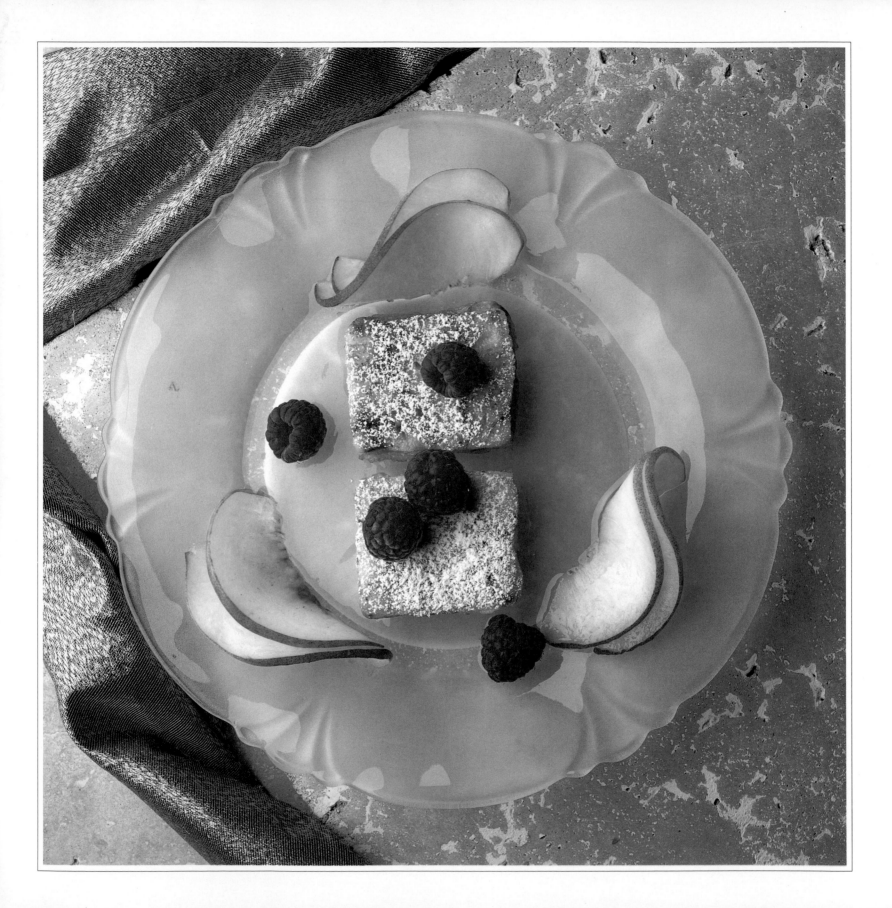

GALLIANO FRENCH TOAST PETITS FOURS

3 eggs

¼ cup Galliano liqueur

¼ cup pineapple juice

4 slices egg bread, crusts removed
    and cut into quarters

Unsalted butter for frying

Confectioners' sugar

½ cup Galliano liqueur for serving

1 peach, peeled, pitted, and very
    thinly sliced

½ cup raspberries

□ Beat eggs lightly, then whisk in Galliano and pineapple juice. Soak bread in egg mixture until slices are moistened throughout.

□ Place a large skillet over medium heat and melt 1 tablespoon butter. Fry bread slices in butter until golden brown on both sides, adding more butter as needed to prevent bread from burning. Remove to a plate and dust with confectioners' sugar.

□ Spoon 2 tablespoons of Galliano onto each serving plate. Set petits fours in Galliano. Surround with peach slices and raspberries. Serves 4.

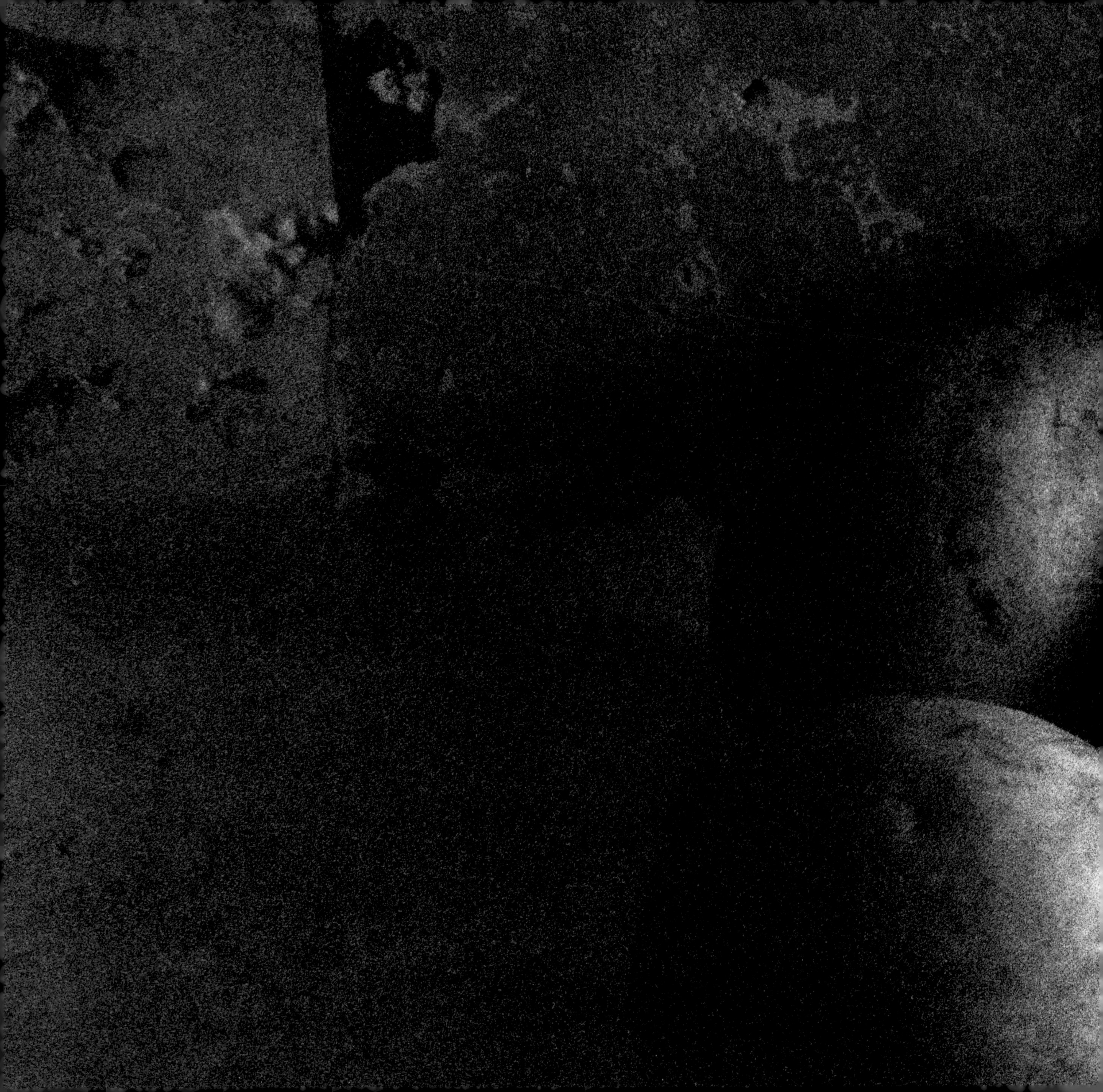

ELEGANT
PEAR DESSERT

2 baking pears

2 to 3 cups Sauterne wine

2 tablespoons fresh lemon juice

1 9-by-14-inch sheet frozen puff
  pastry dough (available in specialty
  shops and some supermarkets),
  thawed in refrigerator

1 organic lemon, very thinly sliced

1/4 cup granulated sugar

1 cup prepared lemon curd

1 cup prepared chocolate sauce

Garnish:

Raspberries

Mint sprigs

Chocolate leaves

□ Peel pears. Slice in half lengthwise and remove and discard cores. Place pears in a saucepan, add Sauterne to cover, bring to a low simmer, and poach for 20 minutes or until tender but not mushy when pierced with a fork. Remove from liquid and drain on paper toweling. Paint all over with lemon juice; cover and cool.

□ Cut puff pastry dough into 4 pieces each 3½ inches wide and 9 inches long. Rub a little cold water along the perimeters of the pastry pieces. Fold each piece in half to form a 3½-by-4½-inch rectangle. Press edges together lightly with fingertips. Bake in a preheated 375 degree oven for 15 minutes until puffed and golden. Cool.

□ In a sauté pan, place lemon slices and sugar. Add water just to cover. Cook over medium heat for 5 to 10 minutes, until slices begin to soften. Drain and cool.

□ Slice pear halves into ¼-inch-thick slices, keeping shapes intact.

□ With a sharp knife, split pastry biscuits. Set "lids" aside. Spread a thin layer of the lemon curd over each pastry base. Top with 2 or 3 lemon slices and a sliced pear half, fanning the slices slightly. Top with reserved pastry lids.

□ Thin remaining lemon curd with a little hot water to make a sauce consistency.

□ Place pastry biscuits on individual serving plates. Spoon some of the lemon and chocolate sauces around the base of each biscuit. Garnish with a few raspberries, mint sprigs, and a chocolate leaf, if desired. Serves 4.

OPEN-FACED PEAR SANDWICH

Top wheat bread with Aïoli, salad burnet, dry Monterey Jack cheese, sliced pears, and toasted almonds.

Aïoli:

4 to 6 garlic cloves

1 egg

1 teaspoon fresh lemon juice

1 teaspoon Dijon mustard

½ teaspoon salt

¼ teaspoon ground white pepper

6 tablespoons each
    peanut oil and olive oil

□ Chop the garlic in a blender or food processor. Add the egg, lemon juice, mustard, salt, and pepper, and process to combine.

□ With the machine running, slowly begin to drip the oils into the mixture. Continue to add all the oil in a fine stream, until mixture has the consistency of mayonnaise. Makes about 1 cup.

Red Bartlett Pear

A pear
arranges itself,
perfumes the air,
and becomes
the perfect dessert.
A.N.

The proud, aristocratic pear persists in its individuality and fussy temperament when corraled by orchardists. It will not ripen on the tree, and so must be picked hard and then watched over. It ripens from the inside outward, giving almost no sign; wait a day too long and the pear will be mushy, bland, and "sleepy" instead of sweet and smooth. This vigil inspires the notion that one may need to rise in the middle of the night to catch the unexpressive fruit at its peak of perfection. ¶ American pioneers wasted nothing of the pear. They ate the fruit or used the juice for "perry," a pear cider; crafted furniture and tools from the wood; and turned the leaves into yellow dye. ¶ One of the first variety lists—numbering five or six—was comprised by Cato before the Christian era. We know the juicy Bartlett, a yellow or red lopsided bell; spicy, yellow-green Anjou; russet-skinned Bosc with long, tapering neck; the juicy, bulbous Comice; small, creamy Nelis; and bite-sized, red-blushing Seckel. The best pears are labeled *beurre* ("butter"), for their melting texture.

WINTER FRUIT COMPOTE WITH BANANA MADELEINES

1 red cooking apple

1 green cooking apple

1 red Bartlett pear

1 Comice or Bosc pear

1/2 cup raisins

1/2 cup seedless red grapes

1/2 cup seedless green grapes

1 tablespoon whole cloves

2 sticks cinnamon

1/4 teaspoon freshly grated nutmeg

1 1/2 cups apple juice

2 tablespoons arrowroot

Banana Madeleines (recipe follows)

□ Core apples and pears and cut into 1-inch chunks. Place in a large saucepan. Add raisins, grapes, and spices.

□ Pour apple juice over all, adding water if necessary to cover fruit. Bring to a boil. Reduce heat to low and simmer, covered, for 15 minutes.

□ Remove 1/2 cup liquid. Let cool slightly. Stir in arrowroot to make a paste.

□ Return arrowroot mixture to fruit in saucepan. Mix well. Simmer, stirring, until mixture thickens. Remove from heat. Let stand for 10 minutes, then serve with Banana Madeleines. Serves 6.

BANANA MADELEINES

3/4 cup flour

1/2 cup granulated sugar

1/2 teaspoon baking powder

1/2 teaspoon baking soda

1/4 teaspoon salt

1/2 teaspoon ground cardamom

5 tablespoons unsalted butter,
  melted and cooled briefly

1/3 cup buttermilk

1 egg

1/2 cup grated ripe banana
  (about 1 large)

1/4 cup ground walnuts

Confectioners' sugar

□ In a large mixing bowl, sift together flour, sugar, baking powder, baking soda, salt, and cardamom.

□ In another bowl, beat together butter, buttermilk, egg, banana, and walnuts. Add to flour mixture, combining at low speed and then beating at high speed for 2 minutes.

□ Fill well-greased madeleine molds to just below the rim and bake in a preheated 350 degree oven for 15 minutes, or until golden. Allow to cool for a few minutes before unmolding onto a wire rack to cool completely. Dust with confectioners' sugar. Makes 16 to 20.

PERSIMMON

BROILED PERSIMMONS

2 ripe persimmons

1 cup amaretti

¼ cup Frangelico liqueur

*2 tablespoons unsalted butter,
    cut into small bits*

½ cup sweetened whipped cream

Fresh mint leaves for garnish

□ Cut persimmons in half lengthwise. Remove seeds.

□ Set aside 8 cookies. Crush remainder and use to fill seed cavities, reserving a small amount of crumbs for garnish.

□ Arrange persimmon halves on a baking sheet. Drizzle each persimmon half with 1 tablespoon Frangelico. Dot with butter.

□ Broil about 1 inch from flame for 1 to 2 minutes, or until persimmons begin to brown. Do not overcook.

□ Transfer each persimmon half to a serving plate. Top each with a dollop of whipped cream. Garnish with remaining crumbs and mint leaves. Serve with reserved *amaretti*. Serves 4.

Hachiya Persimmon

Write me down
As one who loved poetry,
And persimmons.
Shiki

Persimmons ask us to deny our eyes. Firm, full-colored fruit fools us into believing it is ripe, when the flesh is still harshly astringent. The bright, glossy orange-red globe must turn meltingly soft, its skin translucent and even a bit shriveled, before the glutinous pulp is sweet and ready to be scooped out. ¶ Native to China and a relative of the ebony, the persimmon tree is prolific, the acorn-shaped fruit dense and heavy on branches growing every which way. The thick, shiny green leaves fall before the fruit ripens, leaving the gnarly tree laden with waxy, flame-colored fruit against the cool, gray fall landscape. It is known as the possum tree in the South, because after eating their fill of persimmons, possums fall asleep, hanging by their tails among the branches. ¶ In Japan, persimmons are left on the bough until the first heavy frost. The jelly-soft pulp freezes, and the fruit is eaten straight from the tree, like an iced dessert.

PLUM

CHICKEN SALAD WITH ASSORTED PLUMS

Vinaigrette:

2 tablespoons grainy Dijon mustard

6 tablespoons black currant vinegar

½ cup light French olive oil

Salad:

2 chicken breast halves,
*   boned and skin removed*

1 head Belgian endive,
*   cut lengthwise into*
*   1½-inch-long julienne strips*

2 or 3 plums, of different varieties,
*   sliced into thin wedges*

A few leaves of mâche or watercress

☐ Soak 8 or 12 10-inch-long bamboo skewers in water for at least 1 hour.

☐ Prepare vinaigrette: Combine mustard, vinegar, and olive oil and mix well; set aside.

☐ Place chicken in freezer for 20 minutes. Slice vertically into ¼-inch-thick strips. Cover with half of the vinaigrette and let stand in a cool place at least 1 hour.

☐ Thread chicken strips onto skewers; reserve marinade.

☐ Broil about 1 inch from flame for 5 to 6 minutes, turning once and basting twice with the vinaigrette used as marinade.

☐ Place a mound of the endive strips in the center of individual serving plates. Top with 2 or 3 of the chicken skewers. Surround with plum wedges. Sprinkle a few mâche or watercress leaves over all. Drizzle with remaining vinaigrette. Serve immediately. Serves 4.

ITALIAN PRUNE PLUM TART

1 recipe Whole-Wheat
Pastry Crust dough (page 17)
1 cup finely ground cashew nuts
1/2 cup honey
2 tablespoons grated zest
from organic lemons
Dash ground cinnamon
1/8 teaspoon almond extract
1 egg, beaten
10 Italian prune plums,
halved and pitted
2 tablespoons unsalted butter, cut
into bits

□ Line a 9-inch tart pan with pastry dough, prick with fork tines, and freeze for 30 minutes as directed in recipe.

□ Combine ground nuts, honey, lemon zest, and cinnamon. Mix in almond extract and beaten egg. Pour into tart shell.

□ Arrange prune plum halves cut side down over filling. Dot with butter.

□ Bake in a preheated 375 degree oven for 35 to 40 minutes, or until crust has browned and juice from plums has evaporated. Cool before serving. Serves 6 to 8.

Wild Plum

Fruit unripe,

sticks on the tree;

But fall, unshaken,

when they mellow be.

Shakespeare
Hamlet, 1600

DRIED FRUIT PASTRY WHEEL

Dough:

¹/₂ pound unsalted butter, softened

¹/₂ pound cream cheese, softened

2 egg yolks, beaten

3 cups flour

1 tablespoon granulated sugar

Pinch salt

Filling:

2¹/₂ cups mixed dried fruits
(prunes, apples, and apricots),
chopped

1 cup pecans, chopped

¹/₂ cup granulated sugar

1 tablespoon ground cinnamon

1 tablespoon vanilla extract

1 egg white, lightly beaten

2 tablespoons unsalted butter,
cut into bits

□ Prepare dough: Cream together butter, cream cheese, and egg yolks. Combine flour, sugar, and salt in a large mixing bowl. Work creamed mixture into flour mixture to form a smooth dough. Gather into a loose ball, wrap in waxed paper, and chill until very firm.

□ Divide dough into 16 equal portions. Reserve 8 portions in the refrigerator for use later. On a lightly floured board, roll out each of the other 8 portions into a round 5¹/₄ inches in diameter. Line 8 4¹/₂-inch tart pans with the rounds, pressing the dough firmly into each pan. Prick bottom in several places with a fork and chill at least 30 minutes.

□ Bake pastry crusts in a preheated 400 degree oven for 7 minutes. Remove from the oven to a wire rack to cool.

□ Prepare filling: Combine dried fruits and pecans. In a separate bowl, combine sugar, cinnamon, and vanilla. Toss half of the sugar mixture with the fruit and nuts. Set remaining sugar mixture aside.

□ To assemble tarts: Roll one of the reserved pieces of dough into a ³/₈-inch-thick rectangle. Cut rectangle into 1-inch-wide strips. Brush strips with egg white and sprinkle with some of the reserved sugar mixture. Top 1 strip with some of the fruit mixture and begin rolling it into a spiral. When pastry strip is almost completely spiraled, press a second strip onto the end of the first, overlapping slightly, top with more of the fruit, and continue to roll pastry into a spiral. When all of the pastry strips have been pieced together in this manner, you should have a spiral about 4 inches in diameter. Gently place spiral inside a partially baked tart shell. Dot with butter. Repeat with 7 remaining dough portions.

□ Bake pastry wheels in a preheated 400 degree oven for 10 minutes. Cover loosely with foil and bake an additional 10 minutes. Remove from the oven and let cool on a wire rack before serving. Serves 8.

Wickson Plum

Elephant Heart Plum

La Roda Plum

Is there anything
Better than an enclosed garden
With yellow plums and purple plums
Planted alternately?

Lu Yu

Wild plums were eaten at the first Thanksgiving dinner in 1621. American Indians planted plum stones and ate the fruit in season; Sioux Indians along the Missouri River made brooms from the tree's twigs and burned its sprouts in ceremonial fires during prayer offerings. ¶ "Plum rains" are what the Japanese call the several weeks of wet spring weather that usually accompanies the ripening of their plum crop. ¶ Taut-skinned plums are the most diverse of the stone fruits. The Santa Rosa, a tart, yellow-fleshed plum encased in purplish scarlet, gives way during plum season to an array of other varieties, globular, ovoid, and vaguely heart-shaped: Greengage, Elephant Heart, Victoria, Cherry. Smooth skins of red, red-yellow, purple, green, or mahogany are pierced to reveal meaty, juicy flesh of amber or yellow or red. Friars and Angelinos appear in the markets as mounds of matte-finished purple-black fruit, mottled with a dull silvery blue that is carried along the cleft as though applied with a brush. Prunes are simply varieties of plums that can be dried without removing the pits.

BIBLIOGRAPHY

Beeton, Isabella. Beeton's Book of Household Management, 1861. A facsimile, London: Jonathan Cape, 1968.

Carcione, Joe, and Bob Lucas. The Greengrocer. San Francisco: Chronicle Books, 1972.

Card, Fred. Bush-Fruits. New York: The Macmillan Co., 1925.

Chandonnet, Ann. The Complete Fruit Book. San Francisco: 101 Productions, 1972.

Digby, Joan and John. Food for Thought. New York: William Morrow and Co., Inc., 1987.

Dinnage, Paul. The Book of Fruit and Fruit Cookery. London: Sidgwick and Jackson Ltd., 1981.

Drain, Brooks D. Essentials of Systematic Pomology. New York: John Wiley & Sons, Inc., 1925.

Evans, Meryle. "Native Americans: Persimmons." Cuisine, November 1981.

Fielder, Mildred. Wild Fruits. Chicago: Contemporary Books, Inc., 1983.

Fisher, M. F. K. The Art of Eating. New York: Vintage Books, 1976.

Frankel, Hans H. The Flowering Plum and the Palace Lady, Interpretations of Chinese Poetry. New Haven and London: Yale University Press, 1976.

Genders, Roy. Grow Your Own Health Foods. New York: Sterling Publishing Co., Inc., 1984.

Gray, Patience. Honey From a Weed. New York: Harper & Row, 1987.

Green, Jonathon. Consuming Passions. New York: Fawcett Columbine, 1985.

Grigson, Jane. Jane Grigson's Fruit Book. New York: Atheneum, 1982.

Hendrickson, Robert. Lewd Food. Radnor, Pennsylvania: Chilton Book Co., 1974.

Robbins, Maria Polushkin. The Cook's Quotation Book. New York: Pushcart Press, 1983.

Root, Waverley. Food. New York: Simon & Schuster, Inc., 1980.

Schneider, Elizabeth. Uncommon Fruits and Vegetables. New York: Harper & Row, 1986.

Spurling, Hilary. Elinor Fettiplace's Receipt Book, (1604). New York: Viking Penguin Inc., 1986.

Stapleton, Michael. The Illustrated Dictionary of Greek and Roman Mythology. New York: Peter Bedrick Books, 1986.

Tallman, Marjorie. Dictionary of American Folklore. New York: Philosophical Library, 1959.

Witty, Helen. "Native Americans: An Extravagance of Raspberries." Cuisine, August 1982.

INDEX

A note on the use of edible flowers:
Make sure that any flowers you
use have been grown in a pesticide-
free environment.